The power of hope
Giorgio La Pira

A life in images

Text by
Riccardo Clementi

fondazione giorgio la pira

The identification and organization of the apparatuses and the iconographic equipment was handled by Giorgio Giovannoni, Oliviero Olivieri, Stefano Tilli, Piero Vinci and Paolo Gini.

Photographic references
The photographs are, as far as possible, linked to what is contained in the six significant chapters into which the book is divided. We take the opportunity to thank in particular Foto Locchi, Photojournalism Torrini and New Press Foto, Foto Arno, Bazzechi foto, Effegi fotoservizi, Foto Levi for the collaboration offered. It goes without saying that the use of the material published here is possible in compliance with current laws.

Fondazione La Pira acknowledges the support given by

© 2013 Edizioni Polistampa
Via Livorno, 8/32 - 50142 Firenze - Tel. 055 73787
info@leonardolibri.com - www.leonardolibri.com
© 2022 Solidarity Hall

"God's hope is identified with human hope. There is a confluence between man's elementary hope and God's loving response"

Giorgio La Pira

Preface

His joyful spirituality seems to shine out from most of the historic photos in this collection. La Pira the Public Official, welcoming world dignitaries to his beautiful city. La Pira the Consoler, engaging with his fellow Florentines in times of crisis and distress. La Pira the Devout, practicing his faith daily amidst the faithful.

The Second Vatican Council spoke of both the *universal call to holiness* and the laity's responsibility to *penetrate and perfect the temporal order with the spirit of the Gospel*. These are the complementary ideals, lived vigorously, creatively, and with interior freedom, from which lay saints are made.

A saintly politician–in these cynical times, the phrase almost makes us laugh. And yet Giorgio La Pira, a man of deep spirituality, solicitude for the poor, and a longing for peace, is a figure in whom we see the aspirations of the Second Vatican Council brought together in personal holiness and public service. He is a prophetic witness for our time marked as it is by crisis, today with both social and environmental dimensions.

La Pira was a personal friend of Pope St. Paul VI and has been commended for emulation by Pope St. John Paul II, Pope Benedict XVI, and Pope Francis who, speaking in 2018, said:

"At a time when the complexity of Italian and international political life requires lay faithful and statesmen of great human and Christian importance for the service of the common good, it is important to rediscover Giorgio La Pira, an exemplary figure for the Church and for the contemporary world."

In the English-language publication of this text created by the La Pira Foundation, we hope the rediscovery of Catholic figures such as La Pira can be part of a broader effort of cultural memory in the service of what we might call social Catholicism of the last century. The latter term refers to the priests, sisters, and laypeople whose spirituality, focused on engagement with the problems of the world, was an essential element in their quest for holiness.

From La Pira's writings:

> *"Our 'programme' of sanctification has been upset; we believed that the silent walls of prayer were sufficient! We believed that closed within the internal fortress of prayer we could stay apart from the problems that were troubling the world. But no sir! We find ourselves caught up in a series of issues that are sometimes invincibly hard; a situation that tells us that Jesus' cry, 'You will have tribulations in the world–take up your cross and follow me', is not a mere expression of piety.*

"Leave the closed garden of prayer behind but let the bottom of your heart stay bound to it... Prayer is not enough; the interior life is not enough. This life needs to construct external channels for it to circulate in the city of man. We have to change society!"

The Holy Father Pope Francis has asked us to rediscover La Pira. It is our hope that this book will allow many to both rediscover and discover for the first time this uniquely important figure in the resistance to Fascism, twentieth-century Italian politics, the modern peace movement, and the Church of the Second Vatican Council.

The publishers gratefully acknowledge the assistance of Fr. Augustine Hilander OP of the Dominican Province of the Most Holy Name of Jesus who closely edited the English translation in preparation for publication.

January 2022

Mario Primicerio, *president, La Pira Foundation*
Joe Waters, *co-founder + ceo, Capita*
Elias Crim, *executive director, Solidarity Hall*

The power of hope
Giorgio La Pira

The Messina years:
from childhood to university

God's hope is identified with human hope. There is a confluence between man's elementary hope and God's loving response.

Giorgio La Pira

Giorgio La Pira was born on January 9, 1904, in the small town of Pozzallo, situated on the south coast of Sicily facing Africa. He was the eldest of six children—four boys and two girls—born to Gaetano La Pira and Angela Occhipinti. Giorgio's family was of humble origins: his father Gaetano administered the assets of the marchesi Tedeschi, which effectively tied him to Pozzallo, where there were few opportunities for intellectual and social growth, and no education beyond elementary school. For many children from poor families that meant a future following in their fathers' footsteps: a few short years of school and early entrance into the world of work. When young Giorgio was enrolled in elementary school his destiny appeared to be mapped out; but the liveliness and intuition he displayed from his first years at school led him down a different path. His intelligence, tenacity, and sense of duty persuaded his family that he should continue studying. So, in October 1914, aged 10, La Pira went to stay with his uncle, Luigi Occhipinti, in Messina. Luigi was Giorgio's godfather as well and would prove to be a key figure in his upbringing. A state railway employee who had moved to Messina in 1911, shortly after the tragic earthquake that devastated the city in 1908, Luigi Occhipinti had a certain entrepreneurial flair and saw an opportunity to carve out a role for himself in the reconstruction work. Keen to top up his salary to support his extended family living in a shack assigned to him by the railway company in the center of Messina, Luigi set up a business selling wines, liqueurs, oil, and tobacco. La Pira helped out as well; in the meantime, he had successfully finished both elementary school and three years of middle school, before going on to the A.M. Jaci High School, specializing in technical and business subjects. He completed his high-school diploma in bookkeeping and business studies in 1920.

In the war years especially, La Pira divided his time between working the tobacconist's and his studies, in which he continued to excel, catching the eye of his teachers. One of these, Federico Rampolla del Tindaro (1885–1934), played a vital role in the choices made by Giorgio. One afternoon he asked him if he would like to study for a high-school diploma in classical studies, and for eight months he prepared him for it. This enabled him to enroll at university, and to embark on what would be his path in life, instead of continuing to work as a bookkeeper in his uncle's business.

While his uncle saw Giorgio's talent, others set him on the path that became his vocation: Federico Rampolla del Tindaro, who brought out La Pira's intellectual and human qualities to the full, and his brother, Monsignor Mariano Rampolla del Tindaro, who was particularly important for the young man's journey of faith. They were masters for school, life, and spirituality, giving clear shape and direction to the life of La Pira, who slowly grasped the mysterious unfolding of a grander and divine design. This, in short, was the distinctive feature of La Pira's youth: a spirit hungry for and in a continual quest for truth, striving to discover the profound side to everything he experienced.

This can be clearly seen in letters sent to his friends in Messina in 1920–1922: "*On various occasions, and with varying difficulty,*" La Pira wrote, "*I have traversed the underground passages of the mind: I have knocked on many doors, like a poor beggar, in search of the bread of knowledge. I have gone down countless roads, through countless worlds, and I have loved countless things: I have been too much of a vagabond in this ceaseless wandering quest for some peace for my soul: I have always craved asceticism, craved a profound annulment in my essential being linked to God*". La Pira was an intelligent and willing young man, but above all someone who gleaned ideas from everyone he met in order to ponder the meaning of existence. This is the context in which his "intellectual restlessness" should be read: between 1917 and 1920 he mixed with a group of bright, non-conformist friends, including Salvatore Pugliatti (who went on to be rector of the University of Messina) and the future Nobel prizewinner for literature, Salvatore Quasimodo. In those years they enlivened student life with the magazine *Il Nuovo Giornale Letterario*.

Giorgio La Pira at eighteen in Messina

Closely bound up with the continual development of La Pira's thought was his meditative phase, which followed the years of intellectual fervor, and his passion for humanistic studies, his quest for faith, and his studies at the University of Messina's law school. His time at university between 1922 and 1926 enabled La Pira to mature spiritually and intellectually, which translated into cultural choices associated with the reasons for his faith and into a commitment to bear witness to the Christian faith in society. This is how La Pira came to forge new ties and friendships, for instance with the convert Guido Ghersi, a university classmate who introduced him to the French Catholic thought of Maurice Blondel and Emmanuel Mounier in the years of the rise of Fascism in Italy. Others were

Pozzallo. Giorgio La Pira, on the right, with three of his brothers: from left, Salvatore, Giovanni (seated) and Giuseppina. Little Giorgio will leave Pozzallo in 1914.

with Monsignor Luigi Bensaja, the ecclesiastical assistant of the Italian Catholic Federation of University Students (FUCI), who became his spiritual director, and with the professor of law Emilio Betti. The latter was so impressed by La Pira that when the professor moved from Messina to Florence, he persuaded La Pira to go too and to finish university there. This marked the beginning of what would be a crucial period in his life.

But during his time in Messina he had already become a committed Christian, at Easter 1924, as he himself recounts: "*I will never forget that Easter of 1924, when I received Christ in the Eucharist: I felt such complete innocence circulating in my veins that I could not keep myself from singing or my boundless happiness in check*". It was not a sudden conversion, but the end of a long spiritual crisis that had begun in his adolescence and exploded in the following years. And it is La Pira's own words, in a letter written to his uncle Luigi on October 27, 1957, that offer a synthesis of the richness of his years in Messina:

> *Faith— I have stored it up, the exclusive gift of God: here it is, alive, blazing, industrious: put like yeast in the whole fabric of my meditation and action and which has become—as Jesus commands—salt of the earth! A yeast that has fermented everywhere, in all the space of the continents! Despite faults, changes of mind, moments of tiredness, resistance,*

temptation, and so on, here is the faith, bright as the sun, shining in every direction in the world: it is my only richness, my only strength, my only value, my only pearl: but what richness, what strength, what value, what a pearl! May the Lord—it is the only grace I seek!—conserve it forever, through to the end! (...) Dear uncle, I beg you to see our lives from this visual angle, to see the very reason why you summoned me, as a ten-year-old boy, to Messina (enabling me to enter, by studying, the social body and the dramatic course of world history!). To look from this point of view at the entire course of your tireless activity; the good you have done in many directions and for many long years; and the unselfish generosity that has distinguished your whole life. All this is no accident but has a precise purpose: the feast of your soul illustrated by the sweet and divine light that bears with it the Eucharist—that is, Christ himself, the bread of the soul! The time of your formal reentry into the Church of the Lord, into the body of Christ to which you belong by virtue of the baptism granted to you, has come: a joyful reentry, filled with great testimony, confirmed by many fruits. It is the Lord that calls you, with "voices" directed toward you from every direction, to enter happily into His citadel: the city of grace, of peace, of love, of hope—the prefiguration and anticipation of the eternal city.

On the side:
A manuscript page of the digest of La Pira in which are noted a series of spiritual events, often in the form of maxims and aphorisms, starting from 1924, the year of his conversion, until 1974.

Anno 1924

con la mente più chiara
e l'anima più aperta
in attesa di un venire nei la speranza non è mai cessato di
tendere e la Fede mai cessato di sollevare
E sempre con umiltà -
A 20 anni — epoca di luce e inizio di Unione col Maestro —
— 1ª S. Pasqua —

1925 - Ad majora - Spectaculum facti sumus Angelis
1926 - Estote perfecti, sicut perfectus est Pater Vester qui est in Coelis — Sursum corda —
        Adveniat, Domine, Regnum tuum
1926   10 Luglio - Corrado Ferruzo [...] apud Deum Gloriosissimamque Virginem Mariam intercedente —
1927 "Ego sum vitis vera, et Pater meus agricola est ... Ego sum vitis, vos palmites: qui manet in [...]
        et ego in eo, hic fert fructum multum: quia sine me nihil potestis facere."
1927   17 ottobre. Nel 25º della morte di Ferruzo (1902 [...]) Il Signore mi chiama, attraverso la [...] delle facoltà
        [...] fanciulla, all'insegnamento del Nodo romano.
1928 "Si scires donum Dei, et quis est, qui dicit tibi: Da mihi bibere: tu forsitan petisses
        ab eo, et dedisset tibi aquam vivam..... Omnis, qui biberit ex aqua, quam ego dabo ei, non
        sitiet in aeternum: sed aqua, quam ego dabo ei, fiet in eo fons aquae salientis in vitam
        aeternam" (Giov. 4.10-15) Vienna 1928
13.8.1928. O Gesù eccomi pronto!
1929 Deus meus et omnia!
20.8.1929. Signore, eccomi pronto! (S. Bernardo 1929 Castelnuovo.)
25.1.1930 [...]
29.4.1930 A Corrado Ferruzo [...] nell'umiltà!
1930. Expurgate vetus fermentum, ut sitis nova conspersio, sicut estis azymi.
        Etenim Pascha nostrum immolatus est Christus. Itaque epulemur: non in [...]
        veteri, neque in fermento malitiae sed in azymis sinceritatis et veritatis.
30.8.30 Castelnuovo
23.10.30 la prima grande vittoria: l'ingresso al concorso.
8.2.31 Corrado Ferruzo venerabile!
3.9.31 Ecce sponsus venit, exite obviam ei! Castelnuovo
     1932
27.3.32 Pasqua - Quae sursum sunt sapite. Gesù unico oggetto dell'Amore. Quem vidi, quem
        amavi, cui credidi, quem diligo!
7. Dic. 33 Vigilia dell'Immacolata: mia bambola a [...] (colleg. S. Rosa)
2. febb. 34 - Prolusione: festa della Purificazione di Maria; 1° Ven. del mese!
8.XII.54 IMMACOLATA: trenta anni dopo. [Firenze, città di Cristo Re — e [...]].
6.4.58 PASQUA ["lumen mundi! Quale divina dimensione!].
2.2.66 [32 anni dopo! "lumen gentium": "è di [...] cui contraddetur": quale [...]!]
1.2.74 [40 anni dopo! [...] Servus [...] e [...]]

The Florentine years: university, Principi, the war

San Marco, the Convent of Sant'Antonino Pierozzi, Beato Angelico and Gerolamo Savonarola. Hope for the highest values of human vocation and religious and artistic contemplation.

Giorgio La Pira

L a Pira's life changed radically following his conversion. From then on everything was directed towards a spiritual dimension of existence. Every choice he made in his working life found a profound correspondence on the plane of faith. His period of crisis and anxiety was over.

La Pira had embarked on the path of faith and moved confidently towards his destination, which was not established by him but was placed each day in the creative hands of God. This is a necessary presupposition when approaching the biography of La Pira. An attentive mind, in fact, cannot fail to note that La Pira never sought anything for himself either in his academic career or in political life, because in truth he had a sole objective: to entrust himself to the will of God, who always indicated choices and priorities.

To find confirmation of this, one needs only look at the events of his life in the years following 1924, marked by a profound harmony between his religious and academic paths: in 1925, Giorgio became a Dominican Tertiary, taking the name of Fra Raimondo in the first group of Tertiaries founded by Father Enrico Di Vita in Messina. The name Raimondo was chosen in memory of Saint Raymond of Penyafort, a Dominican friar born around 1175, who wrote several legal works: it was a sort of consecration of his future profession to the Father. On July 10, 1926, he graduated with full honors, and the university published his degree thesis, "*La successione ereditaria intestata e contro il testamento nel Diritto Romano*" ('Intestate Hereditary Succession Against the Will and Testament in Roman Law'), at its own expense. Professor Betti held this young student in high esteem, endowed as he was not only with an acute intelligence, but also the ability to grasp the crucial aspects of an issue and read in it the signs of the times and of history. On Betti's recommendation, the university appointed La Pira, a few months after graduating, assistant lecturer in Roman Law. This brought him into contact with young people as a teacher, guide, and educator, another aspect that characterized his entire life.

May 1943: Professor La Pira with some students in front of the University in Piazza San Marco in Florence. Those are the years in which the magazine "Principi" was born.

La Pira's life was an *unicum* in which the private and the public began to merge into a single entity on the path to holiness, as can also be glimpsed from a letter to his friend Pugliatti in September 1925: *"Above all, we must work and hope: and our action, in order for its realization of being, and at once a reason for the growth of our inner being, must flow out of us to reach others and, consequently, to immeasurably expand the boundaries of the soul. This is the zenith of Christian law and the truest requisite of the philosophy of action."*

La Pira's future is all here in these words: work and hope, meditate and act, anchor the soul in Christ and step out to bear witness to His message—both in practicing a profession and in interpersonal relationships, in social and in political activities.

In this sense, La Pira is a particularly pertinent model, at the human level prior even to the religious one. While it is certainly true that spirituality guided all his personal choices, it is equally clear that his humanity was also grounded in honesty and a desire for justice: a combination of thoughts and facts that made him a person of great profundity. He was credible and sensitive to the needs of his fellow human beings, in a kind of virtuous circle in which faith nourished human integrity and vice versa. A special role was played in all this by the Virgin Mary, with whom La Pira engaged in an ongoing dialogue that shaped his whole approach to life, enriching it with an unmistakable meekness, tenderness, and purity. This devotion, never inward looking but always joyfully directed toward the world and to others, certainly helped him in the key steps of his early university career.

In 1927 La Pira won a study grant that enabled him to go to Austria and Germany to attend courses on law by eminent scholars. From their teachings he gained further ideas for reflection, useful not just for his university training but also his own personal maturity. Upon his return to Italy the University of Florence gave him a job lecturing on Roman legal institutions. On December 11 of the same year, La Pira received, again with the name of Fra' Raimondo, the habit of the Dominican Tertiary in the basilica of San Marco in Florence, a place that would be important for future events in his life and which now houses his tomb. This marked the beginning of a journey, or rather an earthly pilgrimage, in which La Pira's human, spiritual, and judicial qualities nourished each other and found in Florence fertile terrain for doing "great things," as he himself used to say to young people when encouraging them to aspire to goodness. His powerful spirituality kept his heart bound to the sky. At the same time, his profession and the vitality of a city like Florence did not allow him to shut himself away in a kind of hermitage that would have deprived the world of one of the most wonderful personalities in contemporary history.

Articulating faith in terms of concrete choices became the prerogative of La Pira, who achieved this state thanks to many experiences and many people, some of whom had a particular impact on his development. It is worth mentioning in this regard that in August 1928 La Pira embraced Father Agostino Gemelli's initiative to found a secular institution whose members were urged to pursue the ideal of a lay consecration suited to the specific historic phase. The sense of this commitment was to act as signs of the times, to read history through the lens of faith and, inspired by this "long gaze," to assume responsibility in the world: it is no accident that, of the first eleven founders, La Pira was the only one who remained in it for forty-nine years, through until his death.

In joining this institution, he took vows of poverty, obedience, and celibacy in chastity, and chose Saint Francis of Assisi as his model.

La Pira with the toga as a lecturer at the inauguration of the academic year of the University of Florence.

Consecrated to God in the service of human beings, a description that would be a fitting portrait of La Pira a few years later. A life condition that Giorgio approached both by continuing his university career, which in 1933, when he was just 29 years old, saw him become professor of Institutions of Roman Law, and by continuing to nurture himself with a spirituality increasingly oriented towards service in the world and linked to works. A key role in this must be attributed to Cardinal Elia Dalla Costa, the archbishop of Florence, who became a genuine point of reference for La Pira. In those years there were long periods in which he went to see him every evening to share reflections and exchange views on what was happening in Florence and around the world.

La Pira "inherited" from Cardinal Dalla Costa a profound love of the Bible, a book he considered fundamental for interpreting human history: "*in the Bible you can read the past, the present, and the future of humanity,*" La Pira would often say. Of similarly great importance to him at that time was his growing friendship with Don Giulio Facibeni, the founder in Florence of a charity that over the years took in over 4,000 orphaned or abandoned children, and which saved dozens of Jews from Fascist persecution. This friendship influenced La Pira greatly, making him receptive to a charitable dimension of faith attentive to the needs and suffering of others, especially orphans and the defenseless.

Assisi, 1934-1935. Retreat for students about to choose university studies. Through active participation to the most diverse youth associations, and through the promotion of new charitable organizations or prayer, La Pira entered the Florentine Catholic world very quickly and also at a national level in environments, for example, such as the Catholic University and the FUCI.

In the church of the Santi Apostoli La Pira invites the women of San Procolo to pray for special intentions.

This circle of acquaintances was further enriched by his relations with Monsignor Montini, who went on to be Pope Paul VI. Over the years this developed into a wonderful friendship that enabled La Pira to move closer to another charismatic figure in the Florentine clergy, Don Raffaele Bensi, who became La Pira's spiritual director, confessor, and friend. In that period meetings intensified with a large group from the FUCI, of which Montini was the national assistant; this gave La Pira an opportunity to learn more about philosophers like Jacques Maritain, whose "integral humanism" contributed to shaping La Pira's vision of human beings and of the world.

Those years also saw the start of the "Mass of San Procolo," which offered spiritual and material assistance to the poor. La Pira himself described its genesis: "*One day in the Spring of 1934, at the home of Don Bensi, we were talking about the poor. Don Bensi said: 'It would be wonderful to materially and religiously assist those in extreme poverty: the poor who are not reached by the charity of the Conferences of Saint Vincent de Paul; beggars, those who habitually sleep outdoors or in public dormitories, poor, wandering people who have neither a bed, nor bread, nor family.' We liked the idea (at the time we were a small group of brethren united by a lively fervor for the house of God!); we had ourselves witnessed, on various occasions, the total abandonment of these destitute people, dressed in rags and regarded, in society, perhaps on a par with dogs.*"

And so, having identified the old and neglected city-center church of San Procolo as a suitable location, the group of friends began to offer the

Identity card n. 4858 issued to La Pira from the Governorate of the Vatican City as a collaborator of the "Osservatore Romano". The document was used by La Pira, under observation by the party of the fascist police, to be able to travel within Rome.

poor an opportunity to attend Mass. The idea was immediately popular, and a few years later another Mass began to be celebrated for women. Those attending received bread, clothing, and sometimes a little money. La Pira described this support as the "miracle of Providence," and it enabled the Mass of San Procolo to survive over the years as the sign of a Christianity which, by focusing on the poor, rediscovered its deepest roots. In fact, this more than the distribution of bread was the distinctive feature of San Procolo: "*Anyone who has known and experienced this cannot stick to the facts; they are led to see in it an instrument (still small, but not without a certain effectiveness) for the religious and social reconstruction of the Christian city. While the world is dreadfully troubled, amidst the terrible ruin produced by the war, does the unexpected success of an initiative like this not point perhaps to the possibility for all Christians to cooperate, in some way, to piece together the overturned order, to counter the terrible manifestations of hatred with a vast manifestation of love?*"

It is for this reason that La Pira used to refer to the experience as the "Republic of San Procolo," indicating a new way of thinking of society and human relations. Standing as protectress over the effectiveness of the project, as La Pira himself tells us, was the Virgin Mary, elected together with Saint Joseph as the "cashier of the work." She always provided, ensuring that the table of San Procolo was never bare.

Dating to the same period were a series of lively activities promoted by La Pira in intellectual circles. On June 3, 1935, the "San Bernardino da Siena" Conference of the Society of Vincent de Paul was established to assist writers, artists, and artisans; and two years later, in 1937, a second Conference mainly consisting of magistrates and lawyers was founded, named after Beato Angelico.

In the spring of 1934 La Pira, with a group of friends, had begun to gather the poor of the city in church, following the invitation of the Gospel "Go to the crossroads and call those you find, poor, blind, crippled, lame, and bring them here so that my house may be filled"(Lc 14:21). Thus was born the Mass of the Poor in the Florentine church of San Procolo. La Pira is standing on the left, next to Renzo Poggi.

These were the years of Fascism, when intellectually honest free-thinkers were viewed as dangerous. But La Pira was neither self-interested nor did he embark on projects in search of glory or positions; his only concern was to do the will of the Father, an aspiration so firmly held that in 1936 he was accepted into the Dominican Community of San Marco, where he was assigned cell number six. This became his refuge, a place for meditation and for studying thinkers like Thomas Aquinas.

A natural outcome of La Pira's decade in Florence was the foundation of the anti-Fascist magazine *Principi,* which set out to defend the value of the human person and of freedom. Some of his closest helpers speak of those years as a period in which La Pira experienced a "second conversion," after the spiritual one of Easter 1924: in Florence, in fact, in a period marked by important new acquaintances and friendships, his faith grew in breadth and depth, moving from an almost exclusively vertical dimension to a more composite balance where his rootedness in God was matched on the horizontal plane by a social and political commitment to serving the

With the women of the community of San Procolo.

community and building the common good. This maturity made La Pira an authoritative voice in the dark period of Fascism, because he was able to sense and analyze the great dangers the world faced in those years of totalitarianism. At the same time, he always retained faith and hope, a state of mind deriving from his eschatological vision of history. It was thanks to this spirit that the publication *Principi* took off. It appeared from January 1939 through February 1940 as a supplement to the *Vita Cristiana* published by the Dominicans of San Marco, the only stratagem for bringing out a periodical of this kind without censorship. La Pira was aided by a small highly cultured group who found the necessary strength to act in a difficult period full of pitfalls:

> *That is why* Principi *saw the light of day at the beginning of 1939. The main, underlying cause has in a certain way been indicated: it was sought in those invisible forces and realities which—according to the principles of the most recent historiography of the profound? (of which the biblical revelation, ancient and new, is the key document)—are the most crucial cause of history! We were at the final satanic turning point of history: a millenarian satanic plan was about to come about. (...) It was necessary—if and to the extent that it was possible—to raise the voice indicating this terrible hour, this demoniacal darkness into which—with Israel and with the Church—the history of Germany, of Italy, of Europe, and of the world was about to plunge forever (if God did not stop it!).*

Added to this deep motivation was another one, also essential: the lack of a true compass—with fixed points, solid principles—to guide historic navigation: the historic ship on which we were embarked was in fact a ship without a helmsman in a great storm.

The periodical aimed, then, to act as a compass in a stormy sea, to convey the real meaning of science and technology as means in the service of the common good, and to help to rediscover a conception of history directed towards the creation of everlasting peace on earth and in heaven. *Principi* set out to demonstrate the invalidity of Hegel's philosophy, according to which the State was the only absolute value from which humans derived sense. It is no accident that in many issues of *Principi* there were continual references to Saint Thomas Aquinas: La Pira had in fact grasped the profound analogy between the origin of legal science and that of theological science in Saint Thomas, the reason why *Principi* was an attempt to reconstruct this relationship between science and the person in a Thomistic key.

This intent did not leave the Fascist regime indifferent, and local officials were quick to suppress the publication and start to hunt for La Pira, for whom a difficult period lay ahead. On September 29, 1943, the convent of San Marco was searched by the Fascists. La Pira, who was fortunately not there when they came, took refuge with the Mazzei family at Fonterutoli in the province of Siena. Two months later a warrant for his arrest was issued in Florence, and on December 8 La Pira fled to Rome, where he remained until 1944; he had to move on various occa-

La Pira at the Convent of the Maddalena alle Caldine (Florence) in 1958 with the editors of Dominican spiritual magazines. In the center of the photo we recognize Father Antonio Lupi with Don Divo Barsotti behind him, both very close to La Pira. Father Lupi, called a "Dominican in the world", after an intense pastoral and cultural activity in Italy, left to become a missionary in Brazil where he died, after five years, in Goiàs. Don Divo Barsotti came to Florence from the Diocese of San Miniato at the request of La Pira. Renowned theologian, he founded the "Community of the Sons of God" in Florence, establishing the Mother House, dedicated to San Sergio, in Settignano.

sions and stayed for some time in the Vatican, where he shared accommodation with Monsignor Montini. Throughout these sufferings, adventures, and vicissitudes, La Pira always discerned the merciful love of God, who never abandoned him, guiding him along the paths of the world. On the strength of this certainty, his return to Florence in 1944 and his subsequent work in public life—from the Constituent Assembly to government service and the administration of Florence—was the response to a vocation that God suggested to him, namely, to be a "free apostle of the Lord" and to illuminate the world with the hope of a new dawn.

Political and institutional life: the Constituent Assembly and national government

Giorgio La Pira in Rome in 1948. Official photo of the Chamber of Deputies.

Is the human city really the hope of man? Can it confidently face the great problems of present history? Can it give work to those who lack it, a home to those who lack it, assistance to those in need, light, culture, grace, prayer and peace for all?
If we turn to the side of God and of the talents, which He, precisely for the solution of these problems, places in the hands of man today, the answer is positive.

Giorgio La Pira

After his lengthy period of reflection and study, it was now time for La Pira to start working concretely on building the city of man. The professor embraced the task wholeheartedly, drawing on the energy and wisdom that stemmed from his teleological vision of history and from his studies, which in the preceding years had ranged from Roman law to constitutional systems.

After accepting the invitation by prominent politicians to stand as a candidate, on June 2, 1946, La Pira was elected to the Constituent Assembly in the ranks of the Democrazia Cristiana (DC). On the same day a referendum approved the founding of the Italian Republic, and the members of the assembly were given the responsibility of devising a democratic framework for the new-born Republic. La Pira was one of the key figures in establishing the fundamental principles of the constitutional charter, and, without ever betraying his convictions, he managed to engage fruitfully with the Marxist and secular reformist cultures which, together with the Catholic-democratic one, had played a prominent role in the Resistance to Fascism.

La Pira had already understood what his "mission" would be in 1944, when he wrote a booklet entitled "La nostra vocazione sociale" ('Our social vocation'), a kind of manifesto for building a society based on social justice: *"Our sanctification plan is in disarray: we believed that the silent walls of oration sufficed! We believed that, shut up in the inner fortress of prayer, we could stand aloof from the problems rocking the world. But no, sir, we couldn't; so here we are dealing with a reality that is sometimes insuperably hard, a reality that makes us see that God's invitation—in this world you shall have tribulation, so take up your cross and follow me—is not merely a pious expression,"* declares La Pira at the start of the text, before going on to assert: *"Don't come out with the usual silly phrase: politics is an 'ugly' business! No: political commitment—that is, the commitment to the Christian-inspired construction of society at every level, commencing with the economic*

In Rome in 1946: from left, La Pira, Aldo Moro and Giuseppe Dossetti, representatives of the Christian Democrats, at a meeting of the first subcommittee of the Contituent Assembly. Among others attending were Lelio Basso for the socialists and Palmiro Togliatti for the communists.

sphere—is a commitment of humanity and sanctity." This view of politics found key support in Rome among the so-called "little professors." Besides La Pira himself, the group consisted of Amintore Fanfani, Giuseppe Dossetti, Giuseppe Lazzati, and Aldo Moro, all university professors and intellectuals who had had dealings with each other while working on anti-Fascist magazines during the war years. Now they were all in the Constituent Assembly, where they played a coordinated and crucial role in drawing up the Constitution.

Besides acquiring political and institutional experience, the group also strengthened their friendship and unity of intent, living communally during those years in a house situated right in the center of Rome.

La Pira became a member of the Committee of 75, whose job it was to establish the fundamental principles of the Constitution, and which was in turn divided into three sub-committees: together with Dossetti and Moro, and left-wingers like the socialist Lelio Basso and the communist Palmiro Togliatti, La Pira served on the first sub-committee, responsible for the "rights and obligations of citizens." La Pira operated in accordance with several underlying principles: the affirmation of an organicist vision and legal pluralism; the priority of the human person over the State, but without falling into the pitfall of individualism; and recognition of the rights of the person and their forms of organization in the community. In this way, he contributed significantly to building the "new house on rock," as he liked to put it, evident above all in articles 2, 3, 5, 7, 10, 11, 29, 33, 35, 39, 43, 45, and

In Rome with Palmiro Togliatti, general secretary of the Communist Party. La Pira met Togliatti at the time of the Constituent Assembly. This meeting was not for him a fortuitous and casual event but, as he himself defined it, a "meeting of the depths that Providence disposes for his own personal and historic goals, of grace, truth, unity and peace". In La Pira, in fact, Togliatti felt the strength of certain convictions. He understood that La Pira represented certain profound popular aspirations, that he had been voted for by the poor, and that he was somehow responsive for these things. Thus it was possible for them to agree on many articles of the Constitution and in particular on article 7; in this light, moreover, La Pira saw in the confidence that Togliatti showed him a deeper, more hidden hope, man's ultimate hope of trascendence.

49 of the Italian Constitution. Several sections in La Pira's report for the first sub-committee about "Principles regarding civil relations" are significant in this respect:

> *If the individual has no metaphysical precedence with respect to the State and if, instead, it is the State itself that possesses this metaphysical precedence with respect to the individual, how is the existence of primary human rights limiting the "absolute" sovereignty of the State sustainable? (…) In this dual crisis lies the essence of the totalitarian State and, therefore, of Fascism and Nazism. What task is therefore given to the new Italian Constitution so that this crisis is overcome, at least constitutionally? The answer is clear: to solemnly reaffirm the natural rights—indefeasible, sacred, original—of the human person and to construct the structure of the State as a function of them. The State for the person and not the person for the State: this is the non-eliminable premise of an essentially democratic State. (…) To give a solid foundation to its legal and political purpose, the Constitution cannot neglect the crucial affirmation of the value of the person: natural human rights exist, human beings have precedence over the State, human beings have value as an end and not as a means because their nature is spiritual and therefore transcends all the values of time. The human being's spiritual and religious roots are the only foundation on which the edifice of natural, sacred, and indefeasible rights can be solidly built. If this foundation is missing or collapses (metaphysical crisis of the person), the edifice resting on it falls into ruin (and when this edifice collapses the totalitarian state inevitably takes the place of the democratic state). To conclude: precisely because the new Constitution of the Italian democratic state must forcefully reaffirm the values of democracy in opposition to the principles of the totalitarian State, it is necessary to prefix the Constitution—as the vast majority of states do—*

Rome, August 1948. La Pira, undersecretary at work in the fifth De Gasperi government, with Amintore Fanfani, holder of the ministry, after shared the INA-Casa plan to the British Minister for Reconstruction Aneurin Bevan, a member of the Labor left.

with a solemn Declaration of human rights. And to give intrinsic solidity to these rights, the Declaration must also affirm the spiritual and transcendent nature of the person.

La Pira's tenacious attempt, culminating in a proposal made during the final plenary session of December 22, 1947, to insert a preamble into the Constitution affirming that "in the name of God, the Italian people avails itself of the present Constitution," should be read from this perspective. The request was subsequently withdrawn to avoid undermining the positive spirit of collaboration forged between assembly members of different cultural and political persuasions. In any case, La Pira's proposal was not ideological in intent, but the expression of a desire to reaffirm the metaphysical nature of human beings and the centrality of the person. The intervention made by Piero Calamandrei, a leading exponent of the non-communist left, is significant in this respect: "*I am not in disagreement with my colleague and friend La Pira; because if the point we have reached in our work had not prohibited it, I too would have liked to see a few words referring to the Spirit at the beginning of our Constitution. Because, colleagues, at the end of our work, which has sometimes been difficult and even unpleasant, sometimes impoverished, let's say, by shabby political issues, at the end of our work there is however a consciousness, a sense of having been part, in our work, of something solemn and sacred in inspiration. And it would have been appropriate and comforting to express, even in a single sentence, this consciousness, that in our Constitution there is something that goes beyond our persons, an idea that links us to the past and to what is to come, a religious idea, because everything that demonstrates the transience of human beings but the perpetuity of their ideals is religion.*"

A Christian-inspired undertaking in its genesis and able to affirm the sacredness of the person, whose realization in society must be the State's ultimate aim: this is why La Pira's contribution to drawing up the fundamental principles of the Constitution was not just about pointing to the spiritual

La Pira with Senator Ferruccio Parri, the first president of the Council of Ministers of the Republic after the Liberation.

nature of human beings but started from that to ascribe profound value to human rights. These began with social and economic rights, because, as La Pira again declared in his report for the sub-committee, *"without the protection of social rights—the right to labor, rest, welfare, etc.—a person's freedom and independence are not effectively guaranteed."* Such a complex and organic conception of the person, could not, in La Pira's view, do without the intermediate bodies and rights of the communities in which the person forms their own personality. As he observed:

> *So, finally, the following fundamental issue arises: when we speak of the essential rights of the person and of the integral system of the essential rights of the person, must we refer solely to the rights of single persons? That is, must we continue to accept the atomistic conception that contrasts single persons with the State in a non-organic way, without taking account of the natural communities that are the inevitable and appropriate mediation between State and single persons? Or rather do we also need to include the essential rights of these natural communities in the integral system of the person's rights? In other words, do we need to affirm that, as genuine civil and political liberty cannot exist without the protection of social rights, so too this genuine liberty cannot exist without the protection of the essential rights of communities? The integral system of essential human rights requires that individual rights and social ones and those of communities are all affirmed together. Indeed, the essential rights of the human person are not respected—and the State, therefore, does not*

La Pira with his friend Senator Adone Zoli: antifascist and member of the Tuscan Committee for National Liberation, he suffered the fascist prison and risked the death penalty. Later he was minister of Grace and Justice and for a short time president of the Council of Ministers.

achieve the aims for which it is constructed—if the rights of the family community, the religious community, the labor community, the local community, and the national community are not respected: because the person is necessarily a member of each of these communities and violation of the essential rights of these communities constitutes a violation of the essential rights of the human person and weakens or even renders illusory those declarations of freedom, autonomy, and social solidity that are contained in the declarations of rights.

La Pira's Thomistic vision of law and of the human person is evident in these interventions; consequently, in developing the main formulations for the architecture of the Republic and, more generally, in the work relating to institutional matters, La Pira and his group also concentrated their efforts on an economic policy at the service of human beings, which, through full employment, could eradicate the scourge of unemployment and poverty, and contribute to relaunching the country. Significant impetus for this came from the founding of the magazine *Cronache sociali.* Just when Cold War divisions were beginning to impact ominously on the Italian scene, it addressed sensitive issues and encouraged a spirit of dialogue between different political cultures. Its innovative approach was based on the view that the human being and the community were the ultimate end of political action. *Cronache sociali* delineated the conception of a new economy championed by the left-leaning socially aware group in the Democrazia Cristiana. La Pira contributed significant content to the magazine, reinforcing the Christian social thinking that was being embodied in the group's

In the sixties, in Piazza della Signoria in Florence, among the people.

political action, which was often at odds with the line taken by the government and the DC.

It was this shared commitment that led La Pira to stand in the general election in April 1948, after having completed his work in the Constituent Assembly with the approval of the Constitutional Charter on December 27, 1947. Despite being at odds with the strident tone of the anti-communist "crusade," La Pira took part in the electoral campaign and was elected to the Chamber of Deputies. The DC won a historic victory, obtaining 48.5% of the votes, ushering in an important period of responsibility for the professors and the opportunity to implement their social and economic program. Fanfani was appointed minister for labor and wanted La Pira to be under-secretary. After considerable doubt and thought, he accepted the post. But 1948 and, even more so, 1949 brought a long series of strikes in various industrial sectors, including the metalworkers, dockers, miners. This was a severe test for La Pira, who was given the onerous responsibility of dealing with industrial disputes and mediating in the head-on clash between capital and labor. To gain a theoretical grounding for his work, he spent a lot of time studying the British economist and politician William Beveridge, whose work was influential in setting up the Welfare State, and the economic theories of Keynes. One outcome of his time as under-secretary was the essay "L'attesa della povera gente" ('The expectations of the poor'), published in *Cronache sociali* in 1950: "*A government which, in a certain sense, has a single objective and is organically structured to that end: the comprehensive struggle against unemployment and poverty.*" These were the opening words of the article, which posed questions for the government on behalf of the poor and pointed out that unemployment represented "expenditure without corresponding production and hence a waste of productive forces." The piece ended with a clear observation: "*these are the specific questions that the poor ask the government: if the government is able to provide a positive response the crisis will be over and the government—winning the blessing of the poor—will be like the wise builder in the Gospel: it will construct the building solidly on rock. If the government answers them negatively then the crisis will grow and the government will act as the foolish builder in the Gospel did: he constructed his building on sand, then came the storm, and there was great ruin.*" The article obviously prompted a vehement reaction within the DC, but La Pira, Fanfani, and the whole group stuck to their position. Indeed, in 1951, La Pira reiterated and reinforced the concept in a further essay entitled "La difesa della povera gente" ('The defense of the poor'). But since the end of 1949 differences in opinion with several government ministers had been becoming more pronounced, and in 1950, when Fanfani and La Pira's further requests to introduce measures against unemployment were rebuffed, they resigned from their posts. De Gasperi offered La Pira the post of minister for labor, but he turned it down. He decided to leave government service definitively and to devote himself to implementing the political thinking he had developed in "his own city" of Florence.

The mayor of those in need: the local government years

Florence, 7 October 1951: in Palazzo Vecchio, the mayor La Pira confers, with the unanimous consent of the municipal council, the title of Meritorious Citizen of Florence to Don Giulio Facibeni, founder of the Opera della Divina Provvidenza Madonnina del Grappa, with the following proclamation: "Awaiting the particular merits of Mons. Giulio Facibeni in the priestly ministry explained in the Pieve di Rifredi dedicated to S. Stefano in Pane, and in the social field for having founded in the year 1915 on 1 June the nest for the children of those recalled to arms for the war 1915-1918 and in the year 1924 on November 4th the "Madonnina del Grappa" Orphanage which welcomed, first of all, the orphans of the fallen in the same war, to which the institute gave a continuous noble growing impulse, deserving the appellative of Father ...".

And human hope? It is clear, it is the terrestrial city insofar as it is a prefiguration and mirror of the celestial city. Because it is the hope of grace, and here is the cathedral, the temple, the monastery, the center and spiritual light of the city; it is family hope, and here is the house, the intimate nest and home of the family; it is the hope of work, and here is the farm, the shop and the workshop where the work takes place and develops; it is the hope of culture, and here is the school where intelligence opens up and becomes fruitful; it is the hope of fraternal charity, and here are the hospitals where charity is exercised; it is the hope of peace and here is the fraternal and active harmony of all citizens; it is the hope of beauty and here is the entire city that adorns itself with this beauty as a wall that embellishes and preserves it.

Giorgio La Pira

Acknowledging the difficulty of implementing all the principles of the Constitution at a national level, the members of the more left-leaning, socially minded *sinistra sociale* group in the DC, though bound together by a shared political perspective and an evangelical vision of society, chose different paths. The Christian Democrat party, in the meantime, basically shelved the policy of structural reforms and moved towards a centrist and liberal moderatism. Only Fanfani, who accepted the post of minister of agriculture, continued to serve in government. Dossetti retreated to a monastic life and effectively disbanded the group he had led, convinced that the path of meditation and reflection was the only way to be the salt of the earth and to influence society. Lazzati returned to academic life, convinced that the key to creating a ruling class and a political vision capable of changing the course of history was to work with and educate the new generations. La Pira, for his own part, devoted himself to his beloved Florence, with a very specific purpose—to tackle what he regarded as the absolute priority for contemporary society: peace. This was not an abstract notion of peace, but something that had to be achieved by sticking resolutely to Article 11 of the Italian Constitution (that "rejects war ... as a means for the settlement of international disputes"), just as a world divided into two antithetical and non-dialoguing blocks was taking shape on the international scene.

La Pira refused to be discouraged or resigned. Prophetically anchored to the Pauline motto *Spes contra Spem* ('hope against all hope') and firmly convinced that labor, bread, and peace were not unrelated at all, La Pira switched from central government to working in local government. It is almost as if he sensed that, paradoxically, his more global project could be launched precisely from something much smaller. In Florence La Pira found fertile ground for translating the Constitution into political and administrative choices: in 1951 he stood in the local government elections in Florence. The DC, in a coalition with the small centrist parties, obtained the majority of votes and seats on the city council, and on July 5, 1951, La Pira, who had received more than 19,000 voting preferences, was elected mayor of Florence, succeeding the communist Mario Fabiani who had led a left-wing council for the previous four years.

La Pira had to resign his seat in parliament because a law prohibited people from holding two posts (faced with the alternative, La Pira said "*I choose Florence, the pearl of the world*"). From the outset his administration was distinguished by two guiding principles that characterized his political action throughout: peace, opening the doors and windows of Florence to the vocation of a "city on the mount" in the international context; and the defense of the poor. This originality of thought was evident in his maiden speech as mayor: "*The city council essentially has three objectives. The first is grounded in the most beautiful and human page of the Gospel: to solve the most pressing problems of the humble. (…) The second objective concerns the city's agricultural, industrial, commercial, and financial life. (…) Then there is the third objective, which*

November 6, 1954:
the mayor Giorgio La Pira and Cardinal Elia Dalla Costa at the inauguration of the Isolotto, satellite city of Florence.
To the right of La Pira his friend, Eng. Filiberto Guala. In the 1950s, General Manager of RAI and later General Manager for the implementation of the Fanfani Plan for the House.
After leaving these posts he became a Trappist monk.

is perhaps the most important: Florence represents something unique in the world and has the major task of integrating today's great mechanical and dynamic culture with its contemplative values. We will do everything in our power to make our city more and more the center of universal values (speech to the city council, July 5, 1951)."

The goals were not independent from each other, but closely interrelated: Florence could keep faith with its vocation to be a beacon and light in the world to the extent to which it succeeded in being, in concrete reality, "*a city where there is, for everyone, a place to pray (a church), a place to love (a home), a place to work (a factory), a place to think (a school), and a place to heal (a hospital).*" On Florence's ability to confirm its place as the cradle of history, but also as a city centered on the person and the community, everything else depended. La Pira himself reiterated this by declaring that "*Florence's universal mission, attested by its civic, religious, artistic, and cultural history, also demands, if it is to be accomplished, a specific and particular policy which can and must depart to some degree from the general course of action of the government. We can make our city a Florentine Republic.*" In saying this, La Pira was not being a visionary. Instead, he wanted to restore to cities their vocation as places for elaborating thought and good practices that could bring people together at a grassroots level and build peace through a dialogue capable of overcoming the barriers of national borders. There was need for an impulse of hope and faith, the eyes of the heart, able to grasp in the best possible way the essence and talents of cities and place them at the service of communities, but also of the world at large, which was impatiently awaiting alternative signs and paths for building peace.

It is no coincidence that one of La Pira's first acts as mayor was to confer on Don Giulio Facibeni (see chapter one) the title of "Meritorious citizen of Florence." It was an unequivocal gesture, offering a glimpse of the

January 13, 1954. The Pignone "case", through La Pira's intercession, finds a positive solution with the intervention of Enrico Mattei and the purchase of Pignone's ownership by ENI.

La Pira distributes milk to the pupils of Florentine schools.

direction La Pira intended to take in his term: the needy, the poor, the "last," were to be the main beneficiaries of his policies. These were directed toward the harmonic development of the city, where economic growth proceeded in step with social cohesion, full employment, human dignity, and spiritual elevation.

Guided by this evangelically inspired conception of the city, La Pira began his political adventure as city mayor, making brave, sometimes unpopular, but invariably enlightened choices distinguished by political substance and administrative far-sightedness. "Not houses but city," was the motto chosen by La Pira to restore dignity and a home to every citizen: he pushed for a vast, low-cost social housing program to accommodate the many people who had been evicted or made homeless by the wartime destruction, or who were the victims of several natural disasters that struck Italy around this time. The housing crisis was one of the greatest problems of the 50s, and La Pira adopted a targeted administrative strategy to identify appropriate solutions, thereby avoiding situations of emergency and indeed often anticipating needs. The building of the new Isolotto district is still regarded as one of Florence's most successful urban planning projects.

Thus emerged a programme of housing, assistance, but also jobs and development for a city that needed to blossom and to return to being the "pearl of the world." In 1953, when hundreds of workers were laid off by the Florence-based mechanical engineering firm Pignone, La

La Pira visiting the inauguration of one of the thirty schools built in his third administration, along with Nicola Pistelli, councilor for public works and his dear personal friend.

Pira sided unequivocally with the workers and intervened to change the fortunes of the company, which seemed set to close at the expense of a workforce of around 2,000. In reality, the crisis gripping Pignone was not a bolt from the blue but built up over a long period of time. In the first months of 1953 the mayor had already written several private letters to the highest levels of government, reporting the gradual state of abandonment of some important Florentine companies and the risk of massive lay-offs at the Galileo and Pignone companies. Work, recognized in Article 1 of the Constitution as an element of dignity in each person's life, was a theme very close to La Pira's heart, and he never shirked the matter when jobs needed to be saved and the survival of a large Florentine firm guaranteed. Pignone was one of the most glaring and worrying examples, as La Pira wrote in a letter to Fanfani in 1953: "*Marinotti [the owner of the company] has decided to close Pignone: the news is not yet public, but it has got out. It is an irresponsible, illegitimate, and unjustified decision.*" Though La Pira pressed national-level institutional representatives hard, Marinotti proceeded in his intent and 1,750 employees received dismissal letters, prompting an occupation of the factory. Undaunted, La Pira continued to look for a solution, remaining at the workers' side and adding economic and not just social reasons to his firm stance. As La Pira explained in a letter:

> *As of now, this is the situation: 1. The Prefect should try to concern himself as little as possible in the matter and should never even think of [involving] the police: we will maintain order. 2. The workers will not leave the factory: they are defending one of their rights, because the Constitution forbids the lock-out, recognizes the right to work, and modifies the private structure of the labor relationship, transforming it from an obligatory con-*

All La Pira in one frame: communication, sympathy, enthusiasm, energy, trust ...

23 June 1952: Piazza della Signoria and Salone dei Cinquecento in Palazzo Vecchio, inauguration of the first Conference for Peace and Christian Civilization.

La Pira with scientists from all over the world gathered in Florence for the COSPAR convention, the international committee for space research.

June 1953 - La Pira with the U.S. ambassador to Italy, Clare Boothe Luce, present at the Conferences for Peace and Christian Civilization.

Mayor La Pira receives the French ambassador to Italy, Jacques Fouques-Duparc, who gives him the high French honor of the Legion of Honor.

THE MAYOR OF THOSE IN NEED: THE LOCAL GOVERNMENT YEARS | 51

In 1952, with Alcide De Gasperi, Prime Minister, and his daughter Maria Romana, visiting the Prefecture from Florence.

November 6, 1954: Mayor Giorgio La Pira and Cardinal Elia Dalla Costa at the inauguration of the Isolotto, satellite city of Florence, while handing over the apartments to families. The new city district, built in a very short time by the in-house building under the pressing stimulus of the municipal administration, satisfies one of the most nagging problems of the post-war period: that of housing. The Italian cities, and especially Florence, were now full of houses. It was necessary to create satellite cities, connected with the ancient city core, but with all the characteristics of new and modernly organized settlements. La Pira's expression "not houses, but cities" summarizes this new form of expansion of urban centers.

Florence, February 16, 1955: The Mayor La Pira with the workers during a visit to the Cure Foundry. The foundry crisis, which began in the autumn of 1954, reached its moments of greatest tension in the beginning of the following year.

La Pira accompanies the President of the Republic Giovanni Gronchi on a visit to the city of Florence.

In 1956, with Don Giulio Facibeni and the sons of the Opera della Divina Provvidenza Madonnina del Grappa.
At the far left, the young priest Renzo Rossi, a future missionary in Brazil, can be seen.

La Pira with Giuseppe Dossetti in the aftermath of the administrative elections of May 27-28, 1956, in which the outgoing mayor of Florence achieves a great personal success.

La Pira with the sultan of Morocco, Mohammed V, on a visit to Florence in 1957. On this occasion the idea of the Mediterranean Colloquia was born.

La Pira with Enrico Mattei, president of eni, at the inauguration of the first oil probe built by the Nuovo Pignone, with Cardinal Elia Dalla Costa present.

The leader of the Democratic Party of the United States and permanent representative to the UN, Adlai Stevenson, with La Pira at the Palazzo Vecchio while signing the city's Honor Roll.

At the Day Center of the popular hotel in Florence, in via del Leone, then managed by the Franciscan Missionaries of Mary.

At a summer camp: the Florentine Committee for Child Care took care of the summer holidays of Florentine children by sending them to camp, to the sea, to the mountains or to the city parks. "Today's children, they are the citizens of tomorrow! " La Pira often repeated.

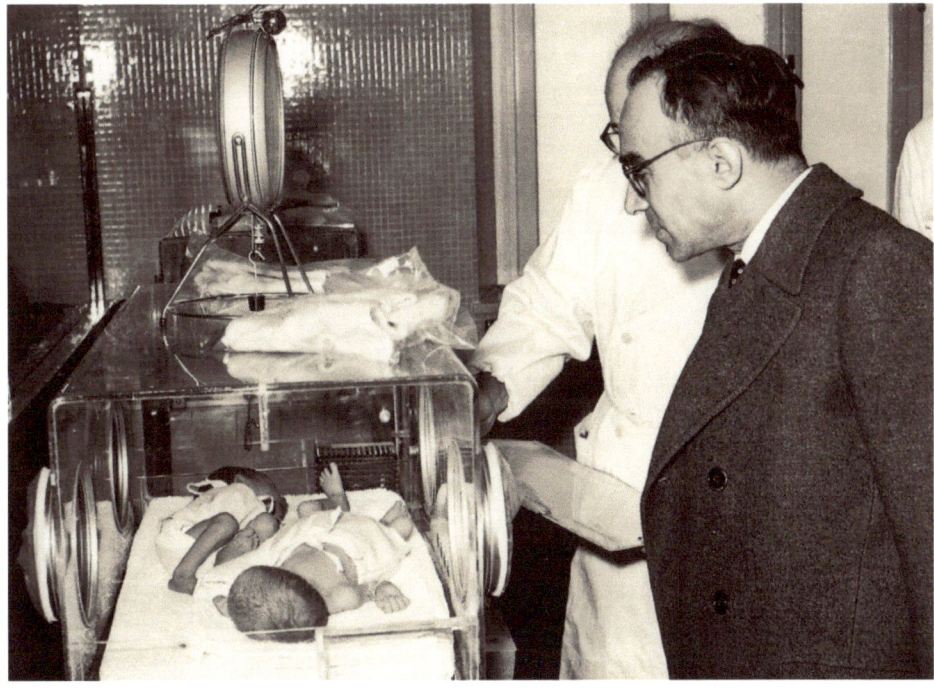

Visit to the Meyer hospital in Florence with Professor Cesare Cocchi.

La Pira receives Prince Akihito, future emperor of Japan, at the Palazzo Vecchio.

La Pira with the mayor of New York, Robert Wagner, visiting in Florence in 1962.

April 27, 1960: the conference of ex-combatants of the Volunteer Corps of Freedom, with Enrico Mattei, in front of the Duomo of Florence.
On this occasion La Pira exhorted the crowd with a curious and charged expression of meanings: "Workers of all the earth, in the name of Christ, unite! ".

La Pira among the people.

La Pira visits the construction site of one of the thirty schools built in his third administration

A conference in the Palazzo Vecchio on the eve of the Ecumenical Council

U Thant and La Pira posed in Piazzale Michelangelo.

With Don Alfredo Nesi.

February 6, 1963: La Pira welcomes architect Le Corbusier for the inauguration of the exhibition dedicated to him in Palazzo Strozzi. In the center, Edoardo Detti, Councilor for Urban Planning.

May 10, 1964: with the Prime Minister of the Democratic Republic of Congo, Cyrille Adoula, on a visit to Florence.

In front of the synagogue of Florence, from Left Corrado Benadì, vice president of the Jewish Community of Florence, Jacob Kaplan, grand rabbi of France, the chief rabbi of Florence Fernando Belgrade, the mayor La Pira and Professor Arrigo Levasti.

tract into a legal transaction that is the source of a certain real right: it is not the workers who are outlaws but the industrialists! 3. The precondition for negotiations in Rome is the suspension of the illegitimate measures of the firm: once this condition is accepted, the negotiations will begin with a view to the only possible result: the full employment of the workers. This is no illusion. The company, due to its size and the modernity of its plant, is currently capable of employing at least two thousand workers. 4. The city is determined to take a stand on Pignone, and, to defend it, will engage in a tireless and unsparing struggle: and it will win… We are battling to defeat a cruel injustice and we will not be without God's blessing.

La Pira's doggedness prompted varying reactions; he even came under attack from Catholic quarters, including Don Luigi Sturzo (the founder of the Partito Popolare), who accused La Pira of being an advocate of statism. However, the people of Florence, Cardinal Dalla Costa, other Italian bishops, and most priests and unions supported the mayor, who managed to turn the "Pignone affair" into a national issue. Even the president of the Republic, Giovanni Gronchi, was drawn in. Fanfani, the interior minister, worked towards a resumption of negotiations to avoid the firm's closure. It was clear to everyone that La Pira had succeeded when Enrico Mattei, the president of the state-controlled oil and gas company ENI, bought up Pignone to turn it into a cutting-edge industry in the oil and, more generally, energy sector.

This gave rise to Nuovo Pignone, which is still (now under the ownership of General Electric) an international center of technological excellence in the production of components for oil extraction and energy production. The "Pignone affair" is indicative of the imprint La Pira gave to his administration: economic development had to march hand in hand with the growth of employment, spaces for socialization, educational facilities, and essential services for all citizens. In a word, a genuinely human city. La Pira battled for it with all his strength, to the extent that he earned the antipathy of certain sectors of the industrial world, of power groups, and of the majority government parties.

La Pira was unafraid to requisition villas and unrented homes to provide temporary accommodation for the homeless. Similarly, when the Fonderia delle Cure ironworks was wound up by the owners, he did not hesitate to transform it into a cooperative and relaunch it. He also renovated the Albergo Popolare, which provided hostel accommodation for the needy. Every Saturday he visited inmates in prison. His whole approach was directed toward helping those most in need in society, working on the presupposition that social cohesion cannot exist if the dignity of a single citizen is injured, and the local council and the State do not act to curb this injustice and guarantee essential needs and equal opportunities for all. The concept was articulated by La Pira in one of his many letters, where he wrote that "*the powerful defend themselves on their own; it is the weak who need the decisive intervention of the head of the single, organic, united city community.*"

La Pira with the FIVRE workers demonstrating against the closure of the company.

Far from being welfarist, it made economic development—where public institutions were in the driving seat—one of the key elements for the community, always oriented, however, toward the fulfilment of the person: money was to be the means and not the end of enlightened government action.

Acting in line with this perspective, in his first administration La Pira rebuilt the main infrastructure destroyed in the war; he established the dairy center, a new theater for opera and symphonic music, and the large fruit and vegetable market. He built schools and introduced an efficient and balanced system for managing the transport network, refuse collection, and water services. Under La Pira, the city functioned well and involved everyone. It was a political project presented to the world with strength and courage with a view to building a world of peace, but at the same time a council administration that responded in an extraordinarily concrete way to the needs of its inhabitants with broad-ranging action implemented in daily life. This was the Florence represented by Giorgio La Pira when, speaking to the international committee of the Red Cross in Geneva on April 12, 1954, he declared that "*cities have a life of their own: they have their own mysterious and profound being: they have, as it were, a soul and a destiny of their own. They are not occasional piles of stone: they are mysterious dwellings of human beings and, moreover, they are in a certain sense mysterious dwellings of God.*"

La Pira had a clear idea of Florence's destiny, and in the 1956 local elections there was a considerable rise in support for the DC and other parties led by La Pira, who received 33,907 preferences, almost double the number obtained in 1951. But tensions in the national government had repercussions on La Pira's second term. In April 1957 he resigned to-

Piazza della Signoria: exhibition of the renewed bus fleet of the Florentine Tramway Company, ATAF.

gether with the whole council because the month before a number of financial deliberations required to implement some important city projects were not approved. As La Pira himself observed, it was impossible, "*given the national political situation and the connection between the political structures of the State and local administrative structures, to have a stable majority on the city council.*" Florence was then governed for three years by a nationally appointed commissioner. In 1960 La Pira stood again as the head of the DC political list in the council elections in Florence. It was a great success for La Pira who, having been elected mayor for the third time, resigned from parliament to resume his mission serving the city at the head of one of the first center-left councils. The journey of the "Florentine Republic" continued, thanks also to the important work done by the mayor's assistants, including Enriques Agnoletti, the socialist deputy mayor, Edoardo Detti and Nicola Pistelli, who respectively had the portfolios for urban planning and public works, together with Pino Arpioni, Fioretta Mazzei and other leading figures.

The city planning scheme approved by the city council and passed in just two years fully expressed the concept that urban expansion should be respectful of green areas and attentive to the peripheries. Among the most significant and innovative solutions contained in the planning scheme, mention should be made of the quadrupling of land devoted to schools, the reinforcement of the network of shops as part of a new organization of local neighborhoods, but above all the guidelines permitting the creation of important infrastructure and buildings for public services.

Between 1961 and 1964 the city council also commenced projects to build a new aqueduct and a large artificial reservoir, which is still an important water resource for Florence and the whole surrounding area.

"Not houses but city" was by now a motto embodied in every corner of Florence, and the 1964 elections reaffirmed this notion, bringing yet another personal success for La Pira. Rare to the point of being unique, it confirmed the value of a politics truly at the service of the people. Unfortunately, the parties were not of the same view. Internal strife was growing in those years, creating an increasingly bitter climate of conflict between the parties in the majority, governed more and more by the logic of mere power. Moreover, La Pira had lost an authoritative source of support, and a friend, with the death of Nicola Pistelli—who was also one of the key national figures on the "Christian Democrat left"—in a tragic road accident on September 17, 1964. On the eve of the council elections, La Pira felt surrounded by the hostility of some of the governing members of the DC itself; yet in the end, maintaining faith with the vocation to which he felt called, he had accepted the invitation to head the DC's electoral list and stand for mayor once again. As already said, he obtained an important personal success, as in all the previous elections, confirmation that his policies had widespread public support. Despite this broad consensus, the negotiations between leading party figures proved both laborious and ineffectual. The social democrats were opposed to La Pira being mayor, and in February 1965, the socialist Lelio Lagorio of the PSI was elected to the post, thanks in part to the support of the communist party counsellors. Fresh vicissitudes, negotiations, and administrations then ensued. But the city had already in a way become the "orphan" of its beloved mayor, Giorgio La Pira, who above all else had been a servant of God and of the Florentines, especially those most in need.

Mayor of the world and a pilgrim of peace

Giorgio La Pira kneeling in prayer.

Why not hope? Should we not hope for the peace of this great human family which is the family of God; the family of the common Heavenly Father! Created by him, loved by him, redeemed by him, to him for all eternity destined! We know: hope is in a certain sense an adventure and a risk: but perhaps, because of the risk of losing the seed, the farmer stops sowing?
There is faith in his act as a sower: faith in the mystery of creation and love that the earth has in his bosom.
He knows that, despite everything, the seed is good, and that the ear will appear luxuriant at the time of the harvest.

Giorgio La Pira

La Pira knew what his duty was toward the citizens of Florence, but he also had the great merit of knowing the city's vocation and the role it needed to have in the world. "*Having become mayor of Florence in 1951, I thought I would interpret the anxieties of Christians and non-Christians alike by placing the city at the service of peace.*" With these words La Pira explained (already at the time of the Korean War) his aim to unite the problems of the city and those of peace. Driven by this conviction, which was rooted in a teleological view of history, La Pira led an administration that was incredibly open to the world: in June 1952, soon after the start of his first term and amid the Cold War, he organized the first Conference for Peace and Christian Civilization. Repeated until 1956, the event saw the participation of representatives from many nations, the Holy See, and leading cultural and religious figures. Thirty-three nations took part the first year, and as many as 61 in the final conference, evidence of the consensus surrounding the idea of reconciliation between human beings and of humans with the community, to then be extended to the whole of humankind in order to achieve peace as the worldwide vocation of our time. For La Pira, pursuing this vocation meant recovering, on the scale of human values, the transcendental value of God's paternity and of human fraternity. As La Pira declared on June 24, 1952 in the Salone del Cinquecento of the Palazzo Vecchio in Florence, while opening the proceedings of the first conference, "*Christian civilization is permanently valid, because the two essential principles that inspire it are permanently valid: the one regarding the structural vocation of human beings for the supreme spiritual values of mercy and truth; and the one concerning the structural unity and solidarity of the whole human family, organically articulated into peoples and nations."*

La Pira also wanted to address and extend a hand to the Soviet-controlled eastern European states, which had been forced to adopt state atheism, thereby denying any metaphysical mooring for human beings. He made his appeal in the central part of his introductory speech, when La Pira stressed the need "*to fraternally urge unity upon nations that have enacted a schism and a secession, to show that this system of Christian civilization from which they have separated is not a closed system but an open system: that is, a system capable— precisely by virtue of the universal breadth of the principles on which it rests—of all the boldest developments that are in keeping with the infinite value of human beings and the associated infinite value of the intrinsic communion between them.*"

At a time when the world was divided into two blocs and was at risk of imploding, constantly threatened by weapons of mass destruction, La Pira saw that cities could play a role that states could not, precisely because of the fragile and tenuous balance of terror. He expressed his firm belief in the value of cities on April 12, 1954, when he attended a meeting of the International Committee of the Red Cross in Geneva: "*This is the fundamental problem of our time, which also has a specific legal framework,*" said La Pira. "*Do states have the right to destroy cities? To kill these living unities (…) of which the entire fabric of human society, of human civilization, is made up? The answer, in our view, is 'no.' The present generations do not have the right to destroy a legacy handed down to them for future generations!*"

October 4, 1955: Cardinal Elia Dalla Costa, archbishop of Florence, and the mayor of Moscow Mikhail Jasnov in Santa Croce for the Eucharistic celebration during the Conference of Mayors of Capital Cities of the world.

This awareness formed the basis for the Conference of the Mayors of World Capitals, held in Florence from 2 through 6 October 1955. The initiative was launched a few months after the Fourth Conference for Peace and Christian Civilization and dovetailed with the whole series of conferences. Florence hosted the mayors of 38 capital cities, including the most important ones from each of the world's geographic regions. The conference proved an effective way of bringing together around one table, for the first time at a public level, representatives from all the continents: their talks were sealed by the signing of a pact of friendship. In one of the most difficult periods of the Cold War, mayors from the capitals of communist regimes (Moscow, Warsaw, and even Beijing) met the mayors of Western cities (London, Paris, New York, etc.). The conference was the sign of a possible dialectic, of a bridge which, despite the walls erected by opposing ideologies and their respective fears, could still be imagined, and that "*Florence—undoubtedly by virtue of a mysterious vocation for mediating between East and West—had the honor and boldness to plan and bring about,*" as La Pira said in his opening remarks. The world was clearly at a junction: on the one hand war and self-destruction, on the other a "thousand years of peace," as La Pira augured, citing the prophetic path of Isaiah, which he himself was seeking to embark upon with his tireless work as "mayor for the world."

Many of the attendees at the Conference of Peace and Christian Civilization had raised the issue of the young nations that had come into being following post-war decolonization. In 1956, La Pira supported the nationalization of the Suez Canal by Egypt, which had only become politically independent a few years later. This position, shared by the Fanfani government and the president of ENI, Enrico Mattei, earned him a privileged relationship with the intellectual and political elites of the emerging Arab nations. When King Mohammed V of Morocco visited Italy, he travelled to Florence because he wanted to meet the mayor personally, and it was on this occasion that the idea took shape for the Mediterranean Talks, where representatives of Mediterranean peoples were invited to come to Florence. The initiative was organized together with the French journal *Études Méditerranéennes;* four such events were held between 1958 and 1964, bringing to Florence many figures from European, North African, and Middle Eastern countries facing onto the Mediterranean, which La Pira liked to call the "great lake of Tiberias"—a meeting place between different peoples and cultures, united though by the same sea and the same desire for peace.

The initiative was also rooted in the design of salvation expressed in the Bible: the patriarch Abraham, the father figure in the faith of Jews, Christians, and Muslims alike, was for La Pira a clear sign of the non-deferable necessity for peace between the "triple family of Abraham," an obligation that the three Abrahamic families and their respective peoples needed to recognize and comply with urgently in order to guide humanity toward the thousand years of peace.

The first talks, at which the Algerians and the French sat round the same table, contributed to laying the foundations for the Évian Accords that ended, in 1962, with the independence of Algeria. During the final talks, in a famous speech on the "Unity and equality of the human family" delivered on June 19, 1964, La Pira referred to the inception of the Talks and traced their history. Then he asked his audience: "*Who would have thought at the time that the massive gulf separating Algeria from France would have been successfully filled in four years later, that the fratricidal war would have ended and that a bridge of cooperation and hope would have been built between the two peoples and the two nations that had now become friends. Well, that bridge has been built; the gulf has been filled, and the seed painfully sown in this room on October 4, 1958, became, at Évian on March 19, 1962, a shoot of friendship and peace!*"

It was a matter of giving concrete form to *Spes contra Spem*, the concept around which La Pira had built his ideas: "*Here is the genesis of the Talks: a tree of peace for the Mediterranean (the great lake of Tiberias) and for the whole family of Abraham, rooted so deeply in the mysterious ground of this Salone dei Cinquecento: a*

The third Mediterranean Colloquium takes place between 19 and 25 May 1961. From left: Oliver Tambo, leader of the African National Congress, strongly draws the attendees' attention to the problem of racial discrimination in South Africa. Next to La Pira, Gabriel d'Arboussier: the last on the right is Bensalem Guessous.

ground sprinkled with so much grace and so much prayer (Savonarola and all the Florentine saints and Florentine mystics)! This tree has blossomed, even if not yet fully: but it will blossom fully—without a doubt—and soon: because the Spring of peace and of unity between all the peoples of the family of Abraham and between the peoples of the whole world, is advancing irresistibly, despite everything, in the Mediterranean, in Europe, and in all the continents" ("Unity and equality of the human family," introductory speech at the Palazzo Vecchio, Florence, June 19, 1964). La Pira had already expressed these ideas in his opening speech to the Third Mediterranean Talks on May 19, 1961, when he referred to the "*unstoppable ferment among the peoples of the Mediterranean and of the world: an unstoppable ferment of ordered unity between the peoples of the Mediterranean, of Africa, and of all the continents; an unstoppable ferment of scientific, technical, economic, cultural, social, and political progress for the peoples of the Mediterranean, of Africa, and of the world; and finally—last in order of listing but first in intention—an unstoppable ferment of adoration, of grace, of beauty, of which the Mediterranean peoples and those of Africa are in some way the repositories and bearers (notwithstanding faults, deficiencies, and errors) for all peoples and for all the centuries!*"

La Pira's vision of the international scene was so clear, solid, and farsighted that it became a full-blown mission: starting in 1957, when La Pira left city hall (he returned in 1961), he made a series of trips and corresponded with the most important presidents, kings, scholars, philosophers, and other leading figures of the countries of North Africa, the Middle East, western and eastern Europe, and the United States. In all of this he was pursuing a precise design that saw the triple family of Abraham and "peace in Jerusalem" as the turning point for humankind. From this perspective, peace between Israel and Ishmael, that is to say, between Israel and the Arab nations, was the keystone, as La Pira wrote in 1970 to the Israeli foreign minister Abba Eban: "[*I am*] *profoundly persuaded (…) that the peoples of the family of Abraham will find their lost unity, the bridge, the path of Isaiah, and this unity of the peoples of Abraham will be the premise and the foundation of the unity and peace of the whole family of peoples! The negotiations with Egypt will succeed and will make peace between Israel and Ishmael the point of departure for a great strategy of peace affecting all five continents, starting from Jerusalem."*

La Pira's letters to President Nasser of Egypt, King Hussein of Jordan and King Mohammad V of Morocco were in the same tone. In March 1957, during Lent, La Pira addressed the following words to Nasser in a letter: *"Excellency, may the Lord God bring, in this period of prayer and fasting, the graces of peace and of hope for all the Earth's peoples; and especially these graces of peace and hope for all the peoples and nations that have in Abraham their common origin of faith and prayer. Your Excellency, you and your people have an essential part in building a lasting peace: that peace which is always the fruit of fraternal understanding, of generous love, of a fecund and fruitful forgiveness between individuals and between nations."*

La Pira, with his disarming spontaneity, with his limpid and authentic faith—which made him seem almost politically naïve though actually he was very sharp and subtle—with his prophetic vision of history, managed to forge a dialogue between people from opposing camps in a world divided and torn by a Cold War which in many parts of the South of the planet had become "hot."

Spes contra Spem, as we said earlier, was the guiding thread of La Pira's work: hope against all hope, bring hope where it seemed no longer to be taking root, encourage the idea of the unity of the human family led by the divine design and by the Immaculate Heart of the Virgin Mary. La Pira's first trip to the USSR took place in August 1959 following reiterated attempts, and it was inspired precisely by the Marian prophecy of Fatima—where he had gone on pilgrimage just a few weeks before leaving for Moscow—according to which "Russia will be converted and there will be peace in the world": a utopia which for La Pira was a concrete possibility to announce to the world and to bring about through a concrete path of dialogue. It should come as no surprise, then, that the day after his arrival in

In Fiesole in 1961 with the Jewish philosopher Martin Buber, who participated in the third Mediterranean Colloquium.

the Soviet Union, on August 15, the Feast of the Assumption, La Pira requested and was granted permission to go to Mass and to pray before the tomb of Saint Sergius of Radonezh, the founder of Orthodox monasticism, in the Monastery of Zagorsk. Bravely and with great intellectual honesty, La Pira—the first non-communist western politician to visit the USSR—raised, during his meetings, including with the Supreme Soviet, the problem of state atheism, which represented the vain attempt to annihilate human transcendence. "*Not walls but bridges,*" La Pira would say, seeing each of his trips as a kind of bridge which, by reaching beyond the Iron Curtain, sought to rekindle fraternity between peoples indissolubly tied by the same aspiration for peace. "*I am not a deluded dreamer; I am a believer, namely someone who tries to found everything he does—like a house on rock—on a working hypothesis. This working hypothesis consists of the Resurrection of Christ and the Assumption of the Virgin Mary, both basic mysteries that move and illuminate the whole history of peoples and of nations,*" La Pira said to his Soviet interlocutors. Though looking at him in amazement, they found in this man from the West a courage but above all a uniqueness of thought that was both admirable and prophetic, because, as La Pira himself affirmed, "*baptized peoples are like birds and fish that always return to their nests, even from far away! So too for your peoples: they will remember the beauty, peace, and joy of their house of birth, the mystic house of baptism and prayer, and they will return to it! And they will bring joy to the Heavenly Father. This is the message of Fatima: in the end, my Immaculate Heart will triumph, Russia will be converted and there will be peace in the world.*"

That is why, as the world had the jitters and seemed always on the point of exploding, for La Pira peace was the only feasible option. His trips and pilgrimages to the Middle East, the United States, North Africa, and as far away as Vietnam should all be viewed from this perspective. He presented to everyone he met—heads of state, mayors, figures with political, institutional, civic, and religious responsibilities—a tangible path to peace. He started from a teleological vision of history to develop a political line of reasoning: peace was the only possible choice, the sole alternative to destruction, and therefore in everyone's interests. La Pira glimpsed the signs of it in the evolution of history, the river of which, despite all the meanders and bends, was moving toward the great sea of peace. Above all else, it was the history of the Church which, according to La Pira, represented a prophetic sign guiding humankind to the realization of the Marian prophesy, that "has its seal in the secret of Fatima." The conclave that elected Angelo Giuseppe Roncalli pope in October 1958 with the name of John XXIII was, for La Pira, a first great beacon of light, also due to the participation of the Polish car-

In Rome, in 1961, during the East-West Round Table, La Pira with the Russian writer Ilya Ehrenburg (left), in the center Aleksei Adzhubei, director of "Izvestia" and son-in-law of Nikita Krushchev (center) and Riccardo Lombardi, socialist deputy, former Minister of Transport in the first De Gasperi government.

dinal Stefan Wyszyński, archbishop of Warsaw and primate of Poland, who in the years of greatest repression had been placed under house arrest. On October 23, 1958, before the conclave met to elect the successor to Pius XII, La Pira wrote to Wyszy ski—who had been to Florence in May 1957—declaring that "*this conclave assumes special historic importance precisely due to the presence of Your Eminence: because you are living testimony that the Church is advancing in the space and empire of Babylon: it is an advance destined to unfold in a broad sweep in the ages to come. The holy history of tomorrow passes by way to Warsaw, reaches Moscow, and goes beyond, towards China and the whole of Asia. A dream? No, a Marian prediction that has its seal in the secret of Fatima. At any rate, Eminence, everyone loves you, even your enemies. We all, then, pray to the Lord for you from the bottom of the soul.*"

The pontificate of John XXIII and the Second Vatican Council were, for La Pira, guiding stars for the path of humanity: the Church was throwing open the doors of God's love to the world, it was opening up and engaging with all men and women of good will, and was reaffirming the richness of dialogue with believers of every people and religion, starting with those of the Abrahamic family. Illuminating in this respect is the comment La Pira wrote on John XXIII's encyclical "Mater et Magistra" on August 22, 1961, entitled "Edificare una città nuova attorno alla fontana antica" ('Erecting a new city around the old fountain'): "This Encyclical, viewed in the current historic context and in that of the key acts and orientations of the last two pontificates, is a historic document of exceptional weight (just as the new historic epoch to which it refers is exceptional). With it, the Church positions itself at the very heart and center of the new epoch and indicates the seven constitutive notes and the seven key orientations—almost seven guiding stars—of the great navigation upon which it is embarking (if it keeps faith with the mission entrusted to it by God): this completely new epoch in the history of the Church and of nations. The seven notes to which La Pira referred, a kind of program for building world peace, were the "*nuclear and space conquest that opens up interplanetary spaces of humankind and elevates it to technological levels of unforeseen dimensions*"; the "*ineluctability of peace among all the world's nations, a consequence that cannot be escaped, the penalty being world destruction*"; the emergence of the new peoples of Asia and Africa, and the advent on the international scene of new subjects destined to have a profound impact on the present and future history of nations, phenomena to which there were also linked "*the mysterious reemergence of Israel, the reemergence of the peoples and nations of Islam, the historic reemergence of Europe, duly purified of its colonial impurities and its social and cultural impurities: a Europe that had rewon, that is, its soul and its vocation—its Christian soul and Christian vocation*"; "*the 'socialized' structuring of a world economic system such as to enable—without violating the original liberty of human beings—the worldwide eradication of hunger, poverty, unemployment, ignorance, illness*"; "*the economic, social, and also political unification of the world*"; "*the unification of the Church, namely, this very characteristic, unforeseen, and accelerated process of convergence of all of Christianity towards its center—at once divine and historic—of unity and propulsion*"; and finally, "*the insertion of Christ in the single new body of nations: to illuminate it from within and to elevate it to the supranatural order (the mystical Body of Christ) to which it is intrinsically (in some way) destined."*

La Pira called this new method the "prophetic hermeneutics" of history in the wake of the prophecy of Isaiah: "*All the nations shall stream to it. Many peoples shall come and say, 'Come, let us go up to the mountain of the Lord, to the house of the God of Jacob; that he may teach us his ways and that we may walk in his paths […] He shall judge between the nations, and shall arbitrate for many peoples; they shall beat their swords into ploughshares, and their spears into pruning-hooks; nation shall not lift up sword against nation, neither shall they learn war any more*" (Isa 2, 2–4).

Following the Six-Day War between Israel and its neighboring Arab states in June 1967, La Pira and his assistant Giorgio Giovannoni went first to Israel and then to Egypt. He had lengthy discussions with Abba Eban, the Israeli foreign minister, with President Nasser of Egypt, with the mayors of Hebron and Bethlehem, and with Palestinian representatives from East Jerusalem in the Occupied West Bank, with a view to encouraging negotiations between the adversaries and creating the premises for a new "Mediterranean Talks" event. This, however, was never organized because the political conditions were not right. At any rate La Pira effectively promoted a form of negotiation and bridge-building between Egypt and Israel, who did not have official diplomatic relations at the time.

In a similar fashion and with the same spirit, he had gone to Vietnam three years earlier: in October 1965—after having organized the "International Symposium for Peace in Vietnam" in Florence in April, attended by English, French, Soviet, and Italian scholars, and representatives from international bodies, with a final appeal signed by La Pira and Lord Fenner Brockway and sent to the governors acting as guarantors of the 1954 Geneva Agreements on Vietnam—La Pira departed with a very youthful Professor Mario Primicerio and travelled to Hanoi via Warsaw, Moscow, and Beijing. On November 11 he met the president of the Republic of North Vietnam, Ho Chi Minh, and Prime Minister Pham Van Dong. Upon their return to Italy, La Pira presented a peace proposal to the president of the UN General Assembly, who at the time was Amintore Fanfani. The initiative was however scuppered after some parts of the plan appeared prematurely in the US press. Peace would be reached eight years later, on the same terms laid out by La Pira. If his proposal had been accepted at the time, hundreds of thousands more victims would have been avoided.

In short, with the Conferences for Peace and Christian Civilization, the Conference of the Mayors of World Capitals, and then the Mediterranean Talks and subsequent trips to the USSR, Egypt, Israel and the Middle East, Vietnam, Europe, the United States, and many other parts of the world, La Pira had made Florence the "dearest" city that "*intuited in these years the key directions [to take]: it tried, and tries—fervently praying and passionately working—to historically adapt to them.*"

Of particular significance with regard to La Pira's tireless work to achieve world peace—one of the fundamental elements of which lay in

On May 8, 1957, at the railway station of Santa Maria Novella, La Pira greets the cardinal archbishop of Warsaw Stefan Wyszyn´sky, primate of Poland. In the years of the most bitter political and religious repression of Poland, Cardinal Wyszyn´sky was placed under house arrest: La Pira had repeatedly protested to the Polish government over his unjust imprisonment.

forging personal and public relations in political, intellectual, and spiritual circles—was a trip he made to the USA in 1964 for a twinning agreement between Philadelphia and Florence. As was often the case in these circumstances, La Pira combined official institutional business and meetings with authoritative figures on the international political scene, including UN General Secretary U Thant and Adlai Stevenson, the US ambassador to the UN and twice a presidential candidate. During this trip, on October 16, 1964, La Pira met Thomas Merton at the Abbey of Our Lady of Gethsemani in Kentucky. The well-known intellectual and thinker had become a Trappist monk in one of the most rigorous Cistercian monasteries in America. The two had come into contact during their common fight against war and the arms trade; a profound friendship emerged from this meeting, rooted in faith and in their shared commitment to peace, and they exchanged letters over the years until Merton's death in Bangkok in 1968 at the end of an international conference on monasticism. La Pira's spiritual and intellectual dialogue with Merton can be considered an important part of his correspondence with many enclosed monasteries in Italy and abroad, to which the mayor of Florence would write before embarking on an international trip, asking for their support through prayer. It was almost as if he took with him on each stage of his peace pilgrimage the strength of hope springing from the silent and deep prayer of the monastic communities.

Giorgio La Pira continued to devote his life to pursuing a possible and ineluctable peace even after he stepped down definitively as mayor of Florence. In 1967 he was elected president of the Paris-based World Federation of United Cities, recognized by the UN. Embracing the motto "unite cities to unite nations," La Pira continued to develop working ideas, make trips and pilgrimages, organize meetings, and attend conferences around

Hanoi (Vietnam), November 11, 1965: with Mario Primicerio on the "journey of peace" in Vietnam, La Pira meets Hồ Chí Minh, president of North Vietnam, and Prime Minister Pham Van Dong. On the left is Hà Văn Lâu, later chief of the Vietnamese delegation at the Paris Conference in 1973.

the world. A true pilgrim of peace, his mission, right to the very end, was "knocking down walls and building bridges," in a period, between the end of the 60s and the beginning of the 70s, when international and even national tensions were running high. It was a prophetic thought, discernible in the answers La Pira gave in an interview entitled "Una politica e una cultura che tendono ad unire" ('A politics and a culture that aspire to unite'): "(…) *The relationship between politics and culture, between purposeful action and a conception of the world, is therefore direct and inseparable. Any politics that is worthy of this name always moves in relation to a vision of the world, of a world that one wants to realize.*"

October 31, 1973 the mayor of Florence, Luciano Bausi, bestows the City Award on La Pira for his commitment to the pacification of Vietnam. Also present: Nguyen Van Chi and Luigi Granelli, the Italian Undersecretary for Foreign Affairs.

The Conference of the mayors of the capital cities of the world, held from 2 to 6 October 1955 in the lounge of the sixteenth century in the Palazzo Vecchio.

La Pira and the mayor of Beijing who, at a time when Mao's China was being ostracized by all Western countries, was greeted with these auspicious words: "The Republic of Florence recognizes the People's Republic of China!"

During the Conference of Mayors of the Capitals of the World, La Pira between the mayor of a city in the United States and Moscow Mayor Jasnov.

In 1956 with the former president of the United States, Harry Truman.

In Rabat in July 1957 with the minister Alaoui: in the background, Fioretta Mazzei.

The mayor of Kyoto visits Florence

On 7 September 1961 in the Salone dei Cinquecento, in Palazzo Vecchio, the twin cities ceremony between Florence and Fez (Morocco) was held in the presence of His Majesty the King of Morocco Hassan II, of the President of the Italian Republic Giovanni Gronchi and the Prime Minister Amintore Fanfani.

On May 25, 1961, the Salone dei Cinquecento in Palazzo Vecchio hosted the last session of the third Mediterranean Colloquium.

A meeting during the third Mediterranean Colloquium in May 1961.

FAO Director General, Binay Ranjan Sen, in Florence for a conference on the problem of hunger in the world.

La Pira with the king of Afghanistan, Mohammed Zahir Shah.

In the hall of Clement VII in Palazzo Vecchio, on 4 October 1962, with the president of Senegal, Léopold Sédar Senghor, one of the most prestigious politicians in Africa. La Pira entrusted Senghor with the task of sending from Florence a message to the Council Fathers in the name of the new African states that had recently emerged from colonialism.

On March 1, 1963, Aleksei Adzhubei, Nikita Khrushchev's son-in-law, visit Florence with his wife Rada and the Soviet ambassador to Rome Semion Kozyrev (who in the photo shakes hands in La Pira), after being received in audience by Pope John XXIII in the Vatican.

Hanoi (Vietnam), 11 November 1965: upon returning from this trip, La Pira will be the bearer of a proposal to reach a solution to the conflict that was rejected at the moment by the United States, but then accepted after another seven years of war, under the same conditions. In a notebook, the day after the historic meeting, La Pira writes: "The conclusion is this: Ho Chi Minh entrusts us with mediation! ... A religious, historical and political mandate ... the interview with Ho Chi Minh: "Go and say: Understand us!"».

Philadelphia (United States), October 14, 1964: La Pira and James Tate, mayor of the US city (twinned with Florence), respond to the greeting of the crowd after placing a laurel wreath on the monument dedicated to Christopher Columbus.

In the United States, October 1964: La Pira with Thomas Merton, a Trappist monk and writer, and the journalist Vittorio Citterich at the Abbey of Gethsemane.

Cairo, 1968: La Pira and the President of the Egyptian Republic Gamal Abd el-Nasser. Since 1956, La Pira, with the help of Fanfani, had worked to get the president of ENI Enrico Mattei to go to Cairo to offer Nasser his cooperation for the development of the industrial and economic system of Egypt.

Leningrad (now St. Petersburg), November 7, 1970: at the Congress of the World Federation of United Cities, of which La Pira was president.

Moscow, 1973: meeting with Archbishop Pimen I, patriarch of the Russian Orthodox Church. On the right, Metropolitan Nicodim, on the left Giorgio Giovannoni.

The final years:
the legacy of *Spes contra spem*

Giorgio La Pira's room in via Gino Capponi in Florence.

Farewell to those memories? Yes, in a sense; because the sweet Mother of Heaven has long since ttaken over, so to speak, their custody: it is such a precious heritage in which exultations of joy and groans of suffering are mixed. And this patrimony of love and pain will be presented to me by the Virgin intact – a sweet pledge of hope – when the Lord calls me to himself on the "Saturday without vespers"; on that unique and blessed day that knows no sunsets.

Giorgio La Pira

At the beginning of the 70s, La Pira moved to "Casa Gioventù," where his great friend and assistant Pino Arpioni was running youth programs (the "Opera villaggi per la gioventù," now the "Opera per la Gioventù Giorgio La Pira"). Arpioni had launched the initiative back in the 50s to train young people. A number of university students from non-Florentine families lived in Via Capponi, and many other young people from the Florence area also used to congregate there every week for a path of training and spirituality. This resulted in an intense and wonderful dialogue between La Pira and the young people at "Casa Gioventù," and with the many others who met at the Opera. Together they discussed the problems of the age, especially those relating to education and spirituality, with the aim of restoring greater depth to the human person. "*Young people are like swallows, they always announce Spring,*" La Pira liked to say, as he reflected with them on the need to rediscover the vertical dimension so as to operate more effectively in the horizontal one, in society, in an age when people were beginning to move away from God, giving priority to having rather than being, appearance rather than substance, power rather than service.

In these years La Pira wrote some fine pieces addressing young people: "*(...) a new wineskin is required for the new wine of the history of the world: peace comes via this path of development: the encyclical Populorum Progressio is incisively clear on this: the rage of the poor is exploding! (...) How can the system be changed? Of course, I cannot say to you: this is the model! Yet some approximate answer must be given. The first is this: convert arms spending (useless, it now amounts to 200 billion dollars a year!) into "civilization spending," that is, into development plans for Third World countries. Devise a "policy of convergence" between the two parts of the world. (...) And what should young people do? (...) It is a new his-*

Professor La Pira with the young people of the Youth Villages Opera at the La Vela Village in Castiglione della Pescaia (Grosseto).

toric period and young people (more than others) sense it: it is a question of "entering the Promised Land" of peace and justice; of building a new suit for the grown world body of peoples." It was in this period, 1976 to be exact—when La Pira, already ill by then and beginning to leave to the younger generations the task of "building bridges and knocking down walls"—that the new secretary of the Christian Democrats, Benigno Zaccagnini, appealed to him for help. In a country profoundly shaken by terrorism and riven by heated debate over divorce and abortion, with a resurgent communist party and a crisis of identity and values in the DC, Zaccagnini thought that La Pira's prophetic thinking could make an important contribution to resuming the right course of navigation, both for the party and for Italy. The DC's enlightened and honest secretary was not mistaken, because at the general election in 1976 La Pira was once again elected as a deputy in the lower house. For as long as his health permitted him to do so, he continued to work to build a world of peace. His illness progressed, however, and soon La Pira was forced to cut back on his parliamentary duties, until he was finally admitted to hospital. Despite his gradually deteriorating health, on August 20, 1977, a few months before his death, La Pira managed to dictate a letter for Pope Paul VI: "*Most Blessed Father, I write to you with the last of my remaining strength. It is pointless to recount it all. The fact is that the life I have been leading for the last few months is hard. The fact remains of a life dedicated to the ideals that guided me every day to this situation. We are now at the end of August, and nothing remains but to reflect on "our fact" and on the desire to go all the way in accepting God's will. Of course, in a condition like mine, one really does not know what to do: before us is the body of the Church, growing more and more every day: what will become of it? We ask this question just as the Lord invites us to reflect on the situation in which thousands of young people find themselves. Pray for me. With renewed affection, Giorgio La Pira.*" The pope replied with a handwritten letter a few days later, the mark of a friendship lasting decades: "*I receive your letter with great emotion. In it I read of your unhappy state of physical health and I suffer with you and with those who are fond of you; and I also read in it your "desire to go all the way in accepting God's will, the painful and wonderful drama of the Cross, reserved for those who reflect in their physical and spiritual experience the sublime words of Saint Paul: "I am completing what is lacking in Christ's affliction for the sake of his body, that is, the church." May the Lord grant relief to this infirmity, and wisdom to reflect, moreover, this regenerating passion in the circumstances "in which thousands of young people find themselves."*

La Pira died on November 5, 1977, on Saturday without Vespers, as he called *"that unique and blessed day that knows no sunset."* An endless procession of citizens, friends, and people of every religious creed and political persuasion came from all over Italy and abroad to pay emotional tribute to La Pira, the "mayor saint." The funeral procession moved through densely packed crowds, passing the most significant places in La Pira's life: the church of San Marco; the University of Florence, where the rector, in the presence of many academics, recalled his merits as a scholar and professor; then Piazza Santissima Annunziata, where, in front of the Marian basilica so dear to La Pira's heart, Father Davide Maria Turoldo recited a prayer and bid farewell to his great friend for the final time; and then the church of San Michelino Visdomini, where La Pira had climbed the famous "steps of Don Bensi," his spiritual guide and confessor, thousands of times, and where Don Bensi himself, who had known his innermost self more than anyone else, performed the final blessing to the departed; and then the Badia Fiorentina, a tangible sign of his loyalty to the poor, where he received a final greeting from his San Procolo friends. The procession then arrived in Piazza della Signoria, in front of the Palazzo Vecchio, for many years at the heart of his thinking and his political and administrative work. Here, before thousands of people, including leading state authorities and representatives from many councils with their gonfalons, he received the official tribute of the city. The orchestra of the Maggio Musicale Fiorentino accompanied the departure of the coffin towards the cathedral. Hundreds of priests accompanied the coffin to Santa Maria del Fiore, the cathedral of Florence, where the cardinal archbishop celebrated the funeral.

One of the most beautiful memories of La Pira is the one expressed by Pope Paul VI a few days after his death, during his audience on Wednesday November 9, 1977: "*Giorgio La Pira is the example that every Christian must clearly have in mind in their earthly journey toward the kingdom of God. The difference between Giorgio La Pira and many others of his time and his world is that he knew, he had the idea, he had aims to achieve in front of him, and he committed his life, his existence for this. He lived humbly among masses of people, issues, dealings; but always with the idea, almost that of a dreamer, of reaching that end. He was a person who had the sense of ends (...). But La Pira left as his legacy the concrete example of a whole life spent trying to 'change' in a Christian way the whole history of our age.*"

In the process of beatification which began in 1986, La Pira was declared venerable by Pope Francis on July 5, 2018. In November2018, addressing members of the Fondazione La Pira, he traced the life of the

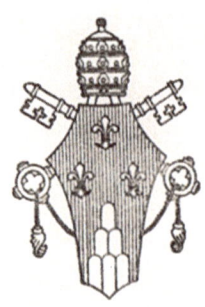

Al Professore Giorgio La Pira, Firenze.

Ricevo le Tue righe del 22 agosto, con quelle dettate il giorno 20, con grande commozione. Vi leggo le condizioni non felici della Tua salute fisica, e ne soffro con Te e con quanti Ti vogliono bene; e vi leggo insieme il tuo "desiderio di andare incontro fino in fondo alla Volontà del Signore"! doloroso e mirabile dramma della croce, riservato a chi riflette nella propria fisica e spirituale esperienza la parola sublime di San Paolo: "... adimpleo ea, quae desunt passionum Christi in carne mea pro corpore eius, quod est ecclesia". Il Signore dia sollievo a cotesta infermità, e Ti dia grazia e sapienza di riflettere inoltre cotesta passione rigeneratrice nella vicenda "in cui si trovano migliaia di giovani". Bene, carissimo Amico. Il sempre compianto Monsignor Rampolla Ti è certamente vicino.

Il Signore consoli e dia merito e virtù effusiva alla Tua pazienza, e nel Suo nome Ti saluto e Ti benedico.

Paulus PP. VI-

Castel Gandolfo, 1 Settembre 1977.

Reproduction of the autograph letter sent by Paul VI to La Pira a few weeks before his death.

"mayor saint," recalling his human and moral virtues of faith: *"Dear friends, I encourage you to keep alive and to spread the legacy of the Venerable Giorgio La Pira's ecclesial and social action. (…) His example is precious, especially for those working in the public sector, who are called upon to be vigilant toward those negative situations that Saint John Paul II called 'structures of sin' (…) As Giorgio La Pira used to say: 'politics is a commitment of humanity and saintliness.' It is, then, a demanding path of service and responsibility for lay worshippers, called to animate temporal reality in a Christian way, as the Second Vatican Council teaches. … Now there is a need for prophets of hope, prophets of saintliness, who are unafraid to dirty their hands, in order to work and to move forward."*

Spes contra spem.

Vatican City, 9 December 1973: papal audience with Paul VI for St. Vincent de Paul.

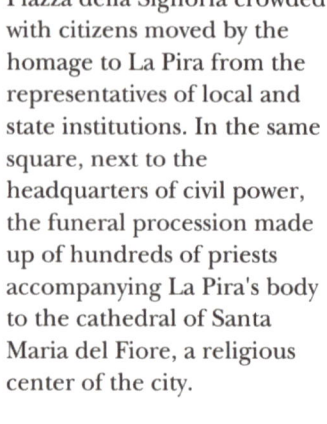

Piazza della Signoria crowded with citizens moved by the homage to La Pira from the representatives of local and state institutions. In the same square, next to the headquarters of civil power, the funeral procession made up of hundreds of priests accompanying La Pira's body to the cathedral of Santa Maria del Fiore, a religious center of the city.

Castiglione della Pescaia, 1972. La Pira with Pino Arpioni, founder of the Youth Villages Opera.

Professor La Pira with the young people of the Opera Villages for Youth during a meeting (1974) at the "Il Cimone" Village in Pian degli Ontani (Pistoia).

Speech by Giorgio La Pira, in front of the Colosseum, during the pilgrimage to Rome of the young people of the Opera Villages for Youth (November 4, 1973).

INDEX

Preface   7
Mario Primicerio, Joe Waters, Elias Crim

THE POWER OF HOPE
GIORGIO LA PIRA

Chapter 1
THE MESSINA YEARS: FROM CHILDHOOD TO UNIVERSITY   11

Chapter 2
THE FLORENTINE YEARS:
UNIVERSITY, PRINCIPI, THE WAR   19

Chapter 3
POLITICAL AND INSTITUTIONAL LIFE:
THE CONSTITUENT ASSEMBLY AND NATIONAL GOVERNMENT   31

Chapter 4
THE MAYOR OF THOSE IN NEED:
THE LOCAL GOVERNMENT YEARS   41

Chapter 5
MAYOR OF THE WORLD AND A PILGRIM OF PEACE   69

Chapter 6
THE FINAL YEARS: THE LEGACY OF *SPES CONTRA SPEM*   93